TOUGH TIMES NEVER LAST

Given to _____

On this _____ day of _____

By _____

With this special message   .   .   .

_____

_____

_____

TOUGH TIMES NEVER LAST

Inspiration from
Robert H. Schuller

THOMAS NELSON
PUBLISHERS

Copyright © 1993 by
Thomas Nelson Publishers

Published in Nashville, Tennessee by
Thomas Nelson Publishers.

**Library of Congress
Cataloging-in-Publication Data**

Schuller, Robert Harold.
    Tough Times Never Last / Robert H.
Schuller.
        p.   cm. — (Itty Bitty book)
        ISBN 0-8407-6309-3 (TR)
        ISBN 0-7852-8263-7 (MM)
        1. Christian life—1960—Quotations,
maxims, etc.   2. Choice
(Psychology)—Religious
aspects—Quotations, maxims, etc.
I. Title   II. Series.
BV4905.2.S35   1993
242—dc20   93–12207
                                    CIP

Printed in Hong Kong
1 2 3 4 5 6 7 — 98 97 96 95 94 93

Learn to live so that your exit is gracious.

May Our Beautiful Lord Give You An Unexpected Surprise Of Joy Before Every Sunset Of Your Life.

If you don't have dreams that are a little beyond your grasp, you've already started to die.

EVERY END
IS A NEW
BEGINNING.

Welcome tomorrow . . . for every new day creates new opportunities.

Get Ready for Tomorrow Because You Will Have a Part to Play in It.

Every problem has its peak and then it's downhill all the way.

C-A-N-'T...
JUST ANOTHER AWFUL FOUR-LETTER WORD.

Be open-minded
—Unexpected
sources of help
come from
unpredictable
quarters.

MORALITY IS DOING WHAT IS RIGHT . . . EVEN WHEN YOU DON'T LIKE IT.

Find a need and fill it . . . find a hurt and heal it . . . find a problem and solve it.

DON'T FIX THE BLAME . . . FIX THE PROBLEM.

Running others
down is no way to
build yourself up!

THE ONLY PLACE WHERE YOUR DREAM BECOMES IMPOSSIBLE IS IN YOUR OWN THINKING.

Courage is spelled . . .

I-N-T-E-G-R-I-T-Y.

THE MOST TRAGIC WASTE IS THE WASTE OF A GOOD IDEA.

Eliminate the negatives . . . then welcome the positives.

GIVE . . . GIVE IN . . . FORGIVE . . . AND NEVER KEEP SCORE!

Starting is half the battle!

Never
believe in
never.

THE I CAN ALWAYS LEADS TO EXCITING NEW "MAYBES."

There will never
be another now, so
I'll make the most of
today . . . there will
never be another
me, so I'll make the
most of myself.

People who belittle
people will be little
people and
accomplish little.

ALWAYS COMPROMISE YOUR RIGHT IN THE FACE OF WHAT'S RIGHT.

Never look at
what you have
lost . . . look at what
you have left.

ABANDON THE "IF ONLY'S" AND SUBSTITUTE "HOWEVER" OR "AT LEAST."

If you're creative enough to imagine a problem, you're clever enough to discover a solution.

YOU WILL
NEVER WIN IF
YOU NEVER
BEGIN.

If it's going to be—it's up to me.

Believe the best
about people and if
you're wrong
remember
this—you've only
erred on the side
of love.

Add Up Your Joys and NEVER Count Your Sorrows.

IF YOU CAN TAKE TODAY AND PUT A LITTLE SUNSHINE AND SPARKLE INTO IT, YOU WILL HAVE TRULY BLESSED A LIFE—EVEN IF IT IS ONLY YOUR OWN.

ENERGY IS GENERATED BY HAPPY HOPES AND KEEN ANTICIPATION.

———

Tough times never last, but tough people do!

Y̲ou can go
anywhere from
where you are.

Big people are really just common people who have simply made bigger decisions and set their minds on nobler goals.

Today's Decisions Are Tomorrow's Realities.

LET YOUR DREAMS, NOT YOUR REGRETS, TAKE COMMAND OF YOUR LIFE.

Inch by inch,
Anything is
a cinch.

IF YOU ARE BOUND
BY CHAINS, YOU
CAN BREAK THEM
AND CHANGE.

IF YOU DON'T DO IT—NO ONE WILL!

Gratitude—an attitude gives you altitude!

Nothing is more
important than your
own self-confidence
and your own
affirmative self-image.

GIVE GOD
THANKS – EVEN
AS YOU FACE
TROUBLE!

Communication is looking into somebody's eyes with the goal of establishing a friendship.

Troubles Today?
Don't Curse Them, Don't Nurse Them, but Disperse Them, and Even Reverse the Negative

SITUATIONS INTO
A POSITIVE
POSSIBILITY.
TROUBLE IS
ONLY
A BLESSING
IN DISGUISE.

The mind that is focused on God's promises of prosperity and power and peace will see sparks of negativity bounce off! We are insulated!

TOMORROW WILL NOT FAIL YOU UNLESS YOU CHOOSE TO THROW IT AWAY.

PEOPLE WHO NEVER CHANGE THEIR MINDS ARE EITHER PERFECT– OR STUBBORN.

Say "yes" to what is right, "no" to what is wrong. And you'll find peace in your heart!

Do you need a
rainbow today?
Then:
1. Expect one.
2. Take time
   to look for it.

3. Enjoy the
   moment.
4. Thank God
   for it. ___

A dream is an outward sign that God is working in your life. Especially if there are dreams to help people or to do something good that no one else is doing.

ENTHUSIASM
TURNS ON A
BRIGHT LIGHT
IN A DULL
FACE.

There are no great
people in this world;
there are only
ordinary people.
The only difference
is, that some people

set higher goals,
dream bigger
dreams, and
settle for nothing
less than the
best!

ONLY THE PERSON WITH A STRONG SELF-IMAGE IS INWARDLY

SECURE ENOUGH TO SHARE THE POWER.

———

THE ME I SEE IS
THE ME I'LL BE. IF I
CANNOT SEE IT, I
WILL NEVER BE IT.
UNTIL I BELIEVE IT, I
WILL NEVER
ACHIEVE IT!

RISKS ARE CHALLENGES TO MEET— NOT EXCUSES FOR BACKING OUT AND QUITTING.

There is in every
human being the
child that remains
within us. The
child-quality within us

never leaves us, nor
should it. For then we
cease to enjoy the
childlike quality
of wonder.

The demanding person runs into resistance. The defeated person runs into indifference. The dedicated person runs into help.